Economics

Revision Guide

GCE/GCSE/IGCSE, O & As Level, CIE/EDEXCEL/AQA

HASSAAN AHMAD

DEDICATION

I dedicate this book to my father "Hafiz Ahmad Tabassum", who has always been my inspiration and guidance in every matter of my life. May God bless him ever.

CONTENTS

ACKNOWLEDGMENTS

Thanks for my friends and partners Mr. Bilal, Mr. Farhan, for their support and guidance in the course of publishing this book. Without this support this would be very difficult for me to publish this book at larger platform.

The Economic Problem

Important Definitions:

Needs:

The things without which, we cannot live. For example water, air, food etc.

Wants:

The things without which, we can live. For example Mc. Donald foods, Branded shirts etc.

Goods:

Goods means the physical things which satisfy peoples wants.

Services

It means non-physical things which satisfy people's wants. For example banking, insurance, transportation.

Economic Problem:

This term refers to a situation that in this world we have unlimited wants but we don't have enough resources to satisfy all of our wants.

Scarcity:

This term is used to describe the shortage of resources in this world to satisfy all of our wants.

Resources:

Resources refer to all those goods and services which can satisfy our wants. For example forests, crops, labour, capital, machinery, fruits and vegetables etc.

Choice:

Choice is the solution of economic problem, that is we can satisfy maximum of our wants with limited resources by choosing more important from our wants. We can explain this in this way that if we have 10 $ and we can buy two things chocolate and juice. We will choose that option which is more important for us. It means we have utilized our 10$ more satisfactory.

Production Possibility Curve

PPC or Production Possibility curve is a curve which shows the maximum level of production of two products or two groups of products from the utilization of maximum available resources of the country. PPC shows that by using all the available certain quantity of one or other good may be produced or on the curve which shows different combinations of the two goods. Reference to the following fig of a sample PPC, we can see that there are different points which shows different combinations of the production. Points A, B and C are on the curve, which are the maximum possible possibility of production while the point D is a level of production which shows under production. And the point E is over production.

Points A, B, C - - - - - - - - are desirable and attainable

Point D - - - - - - - - - - - - is attainable but not desirable

Point E - - - - - - - - - - - - - is desirable but not attainable

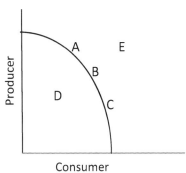

Opportunity cost:

When we choose between different alternatives for example we choose chocolate rather than juice, it means we forgo the benefits of juice at the same time. So the thing we forgo is the opportunity cost of choosing the one.

This concept is of very importance as in our daily life we all come across this opportunity cost in every matter and decision of life. Here is how it is used in our daily life,

Opportunity Cost in different scenarios

Opportunity Cost and Govt.

Govt. has to make choice between the two alternative in its every decision and is suffered by opportunity cost. For Example At a piece of land govt. have to choose whether to build a school or hospital, or it may be to choose between building a road or making it an agricultural land.

Opportunity Cost and Individual

Every individual is also facing opportunity cost in its daily life in its every decision. For Example to buy food from KFC or Mc Donald. In the same way, deciding to do a job or to start its own business. Whatever it forgoes is the opportunity cost of choosing the other one.

Opportunity cost and Production Possibility Curve

In Production possibility curve when the production level is chosen from one point to other but on the curve there is always opportunity cost involved, For

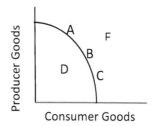

Example Moving from point A to B certain quantity of capital goods is forgone to get more consumer goods. So any movement on the curve will involve opportunity cost. But a movement from a point inside the curve towards the curve will not involve opportunity cost.

Economics:

Economics is the knowledge which tells us how to deal with economic problem and its related matters.

Free goods

Free goods are those goods which are available freely and in unlimited quantity like air etc.

The Language of Economics

Economy

Economy refers to an area where goods and services are being produced. This area can be of any size with any number of people.

Production

Production is an activity through which goods and services are produced.

Producer

Producer is a person or a company who make goods and services.

Consumption

Consumption is using up of goods and services by the people to satisfy their wants.

Consumer

Consumer is a person, who uses up goods and services to satisfy his wants.

Consumption expenditure

The amount of money spent to buy goods and services by consumer is called consumption expenditure.

Market

Market is a group of people who get together to exchange goods and services with each other. With the improvement in technology people don't need to get together at some place rather they can easily do this exchange via telephone or other communication media. Market can be of any type regarding the referred area. For example Local market, national market, world market or international market.

Factors of production

We have scarce resources to satisfy our wants. These resources are of 4 types Land, Labor, Capital and Enterprise.

Land

Everything which we get from earth for example forest timber, minerals, fruits, crops, marble etc is simply referred as Land.

Labour

The people who work with hand or mind and provide physical and mental efforts to make goods and services by using land resources are called labour.

Capital

To make goods and services we need machines or tools we can make these things as man-made resources. These man-made resources are called capital.

Enterprise

Business know-how or the ability to run a production process is called Enterprise. The people who have enterprise and can control and manage firms are called entrepreneurs.

Types of goods

Consumer goods

Goods which are directly consumed by the people to satisfy their wants. Consumer goods may be of two types DURABLE (Last longer) or NON-DURABLE (Do not last longer).

Capital goods

Those goods which are used to make or produce other goods are called capital goods. For example machinery, factory building, office, bus, power station etc.

Public goods

These goods are those goods which are provided by the government as private individuals will not produce them as these goods are not profitable for them. Or we can say people will pay for those goods so producers will not produce these goods. So government will have to produce them and provide to people. For example street lights, roads etc.

Merit goods

Sometime government provides such goods which it thinks

people should have. For example education and health. People may not be willing to get these goods or maybe they cannot afford to pay them.

What factors of production earn?

Land:

Land is paid rent when it is used to produce goods.

Labour:

Labour is paid wages and salaries in return of their efforts to make goods and services.

Capital:

Capital may be paid interest or rent when it is used to make goods and services.

Entrepreneur

Entrepreneur earns profit in return of its managing the business and taking risk of loss.

Private Wealth

All the belongings which an individual owns, for example car, bike, jewelry, cash, tv, house etc are collectively called as his wealth.

Public wealth:.

All the belongings which a government owns are collectively called as public wealth. Public wealth includes dams, roads, buildings, weapons, power houses etc.

Social wealth

All the things owned by individuals and government collectively called as social wealth.

Income

It is what a factor of production earns in return of its utilization. For example labour earns wages or salaries etc. Income is divided into two types earned income and un-earned income.

Earned Income

It is money paid to the people or labour who did make efforts to make goods and services.

Un-Earned income

It is money gained by owning an asset or wealth. There is no work is done to earn this. For example interest received on saving in bank, winning a lottery, having gift from someone etc.

Gross Domestic Product (GDP)

It is the total output of goods and services in a country. It measures the national income of the country.

Public Sector

It refers to all business and organizations owned and controlled by the government.

Private Sector

It refers to all business and organizations owned and controlled by the general public.

Economic Systems

Resource allocation – (What, how and for whom to produce)

If we consider whole country and think about this, we will find that in our country we have amount of resources in the shape of four factors of production and we have to make goods and services for the people of country to satisfy their want. Now we will have to decide that what should we produce and how it will be produced and for whom it will be produced. These 3 questions are very important.

These three decisions may be taken by the people or by the government or by the contribution of both. Simple is that the decision of these three questions is called resource allocation.

Economic systems

A system or method through which resources are allocated is called economic system. There are three types of economic systems.

❖ Market economic system
❖ Planned economic systems
❖ Mixed economic systems.

Free Market Economic System:

This is the system in which only general public is involved in deciding resource allocation i.e what to produce, how to produce and for whom to produce. This is done by demand and supply of the goods. Demand by the public shows that what and how much goods are to be produced. There is no involvement of government in this process. This process of deciding resources allocation through demand and supply forces is called **Price**

Mechanism.

Advantages:

* ❖ Quick response to peoples wants.
* ❖ Wide variety of goods and services
* ❖ Encouragement of using new and better methods and machines to produce goods and services
* ❖ No need to employ people to decide resource allocation.
* ❖ More competition between producers which result in better quality and low prices
* ❖ Profit motive encourages producers

Disadvantages

* ❖ Certain goods and services may not be provided
* ❖ Harmful goods and services may be produced
* ❖ Harmful effects of production to society may be ignored
* ❖ There may be exploitation of employees by producers

Planned Economic System

In this system the decisions of allocating resources are made solely by the government. There is no interference of general public or demand and supply forces. Government decides what to produce, how to produce and for whom to produce.

Advantages:

* ❖ Government provides those goods and services which individual firms cannot provide as they will not get profits.
* ❖ Producers cannot exploit employees.
* ❖ Everyone can get equal share of income
* ❖ Everyone is provided with all necessities of life

Disadvantages:

* ❖ Poor quality of goods and services are provided. Due to no profit incentive producers lose interest in making good quality goods.
* ❖ Government cannot allocate resources accurately.

- ❖ Limited variety of goods and services so people have less choice
- ❖ Mostly wastage of resources occurred in planned economies
- ❖ Lack of profit incentive for producers

Mixed Economic System

In this economic system both government and general public take part to decide resources allocation i.e. what to produce, how to produce and for whom to produce. Mostly resources allocation is decided by the general public through demand and supply forces. Government only interferes when it is needed to correct the malfunctioning of system. For example government will interfere only when there is malfunctioning of demand and supply forces to decide resource allocation.

Advantages:

- ❖ The situation where demand and supply forces failed to allocate resources then government interferes and can overcome this situation.
- ❖ Externalities are also taken care in the process of resource allocation.
- ❖ Many goods and services which private sector cannot provide, may be provided by the government.
- ❖ Monopolies can be restricted to be formed.
- ❖ Competition in the producers is assured
- ❖ Exploitation of labour by employers can be restricted

Disadvantages

- ❖ Sometime government may be failed to interfere in time to stop the undesirable effect of economic functions.
- ❖ There are always undesirable effects of government actions along with the desirable effects. It means when government adopt some kind of policy it has to forgo some other benefits.
- ❖ Governments some time have to take decisions on political basis which are not economical.

Less Developed Economies (LDC)

Less developed countries or economies are those countries which has following features,

* High birth rate
* Low death rate
* Low living standard
* Low literacy rate
* Dependency on primary sector and there is a small secondary sector and very little tertiary sector.

The countries with the above features are called as less developed countries or economies.

How can LDCs be improved

* By investing more in machinery and technology
* By Foreign aid
* By Food aid
* By Increasing literacy rate
* By Improving health facilities
* By Increasing family planning awareness
* By training people and teaching them new skills

Production

Production

Production is any activity designed to make goods and services for the satisfaction of people.

Producer

The person, who make goods and services is called producer.

Consumption

Using up goods and services to satisfy wants is called consumption.

Consumer

The person, who consume or use goods and services to satisfy its wants is called consumer.

Consumption Expenditure

The money spent to buy consumer goods and services to satisfy wants is called consumption expenditure.

Production

Aims of firms/businesses

A business is run by its owners for the following reasons,

Profit making

The main aim of the firm or business is to earn profits for its owners. Business make and provide goods and services to people and earn profit in return.

Pure Profit

If a person can do a job and can earn $1000 in a month, but he rather do business and earn profit of $10,000. In the economists point of view his pure profit is $9000 which he earns over and above its other alternative which he has forgone.

Growth of business

A business's aim may be growth when it is already earning handsome profits. Business's owners may want to increase their sales and so profits. They will try to grow their business in terms of production and sales and market share.

Survival

In the periods of economic recession when demand of goods and services is falling and prices of goods are falling, a business may aim to only survive in this situation.

Providing services and charity work

A successful business which is doing good business may aim to provide extra services to community and society.

Different Time Periods in Businesses

Momentary Run

It is a time period in which all factors of production cannot be changed and therefore production level cannot be increased. This time period is very small i.e. from one day to a few days.

Short Run

It is a time period in which only labour and raw materials can be increased to increase the level of production. Capital (factor of production) will be fixed in supply and cannot be increased. This time period may from a few days to few months depending on the nature of product and business.

Long Run

It is the time period in which all factors of productions can be increased and so production level can be increased on permanent basis. This time period may be of a few months to few years depending on the nature of product and business.

Different Production Terms

Law of diminishing returns

This law states that in short run where there is one factor of production is in fixed supply like capital, than any increase in other factors of production will increase the total production but at a reducing rate.

Productivity

IT refers to the output per labor unit or machine hour. It can be calculated by dividing total product on total number of labour or machine hour.

$$Productivity = \frac{\text{Total Output}}{\text{Total No of Labour}}$$

Average Product:

This refers to per unit of labor productivity i.e.

$$Average\ Product = \frac{\text{Total Output}}{\text{Total No of Labour}}$$

Marginal Product:

It refers to a change in total product with respect to change in unit of labour.

$$Marginal\ Product = \frac{\text{Change in total output}}{\text{Change in labour units}}$$

Costs of production:

Fixed Cost:

It refers to those costs which do not change with the level of production. For example rent of factory. It has to be paid whether we are producing any good or not.

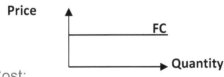

Variable Cost:

It refers to those costs which do change with the level of production. For example raw materials etc, raw material will be used as much as we make goods.

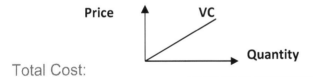

Total Cost:

By adding variable cost and fixed cost we get total cost. i.e. *(TC=FC+VC)*. When we draw total cost curve we get an upward sloping curve which starts from the level of fixed cost because at zero production still fixed cost has to be paid so at this point total cost is also the same as fixed cost.

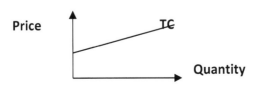

Average Cost

Average cost is per unit cost. i.e. $AC = \frac{\text{Total Cost}}{\text{Total Units}}$. If we draw average cost curve we will see as production increases average cost falls but to a limit then it again start rising.

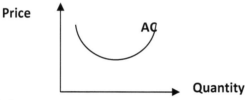

Marginal Cost:

It is the change in total cost divided by change in number of units produced. i.e.

$$MC = \frac{\text{Change in total cost}}{\text{Change in No of units produced}}$$

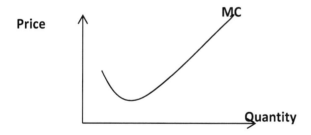

Breakeven Analysis

Breakeven Level of production:

It is that level of production where business in a state of no profit and no loss. i.e. business is covering all its costs. Production below this level is not desirable as business will be incurring losses. It's an analysis of our cost and revenues that what level of products we must make and sell to avoid any loss and meet our costs. Breakeven level of production can be calculated through the following formula.

Breakeven level of production (Units) $= \dfrac{\text{Total Fixed Cost}}{\text{Contribution per unit}}$

And

Contribution per unit = sale price per unit – variable cost per unit

Breakeven Chart

In breakeven chart we draw total cost and total revenue curves together, we get breakeven level of production where total cost curve cuts total revenue curve. This is the point where cost and revenues are equal and business is in a position of no profit and no loss. This chart gives us a graphical presentation of breakeven level of production.

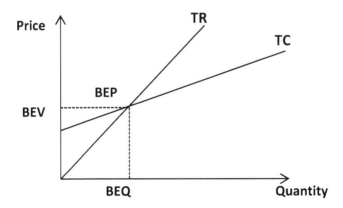

How to Calculate Breakeven

BEQ (Breakeven Quantity) $= \dfrac{TFC\ (Total\ Fixed\ Cost)}{Contribution\ per\ unit}$

Contribution per unit = SP (Sale price) – VC (Variable Cost)

Breakeven Value = BEQ x SP

Advantages of Breakeven charts

- ❖ Managers are able to find out from the graph the expected profits or losses at any level of output.
- ❖ The impact of different business decisions can be seen on these graphs by re-drawing them with different levels and costs and revenues.
- ❖ Managers and owners are aware of their minimum level of production below which they must not produce goods because it will make losses for business.
- ❖ This chart can be used to find the safety margin at a certain level of production and sales.

Disadvantages of Breakeven analysis

- ❖ Breakeven charts are drawn on assumption that all goods produced are actually sold. While in reality there is possibility that stocks may not be sold to that level.
- ❖ Fixed cost not always fixed as if business decides to double the production then fixed cost may also be double. So at different levels of productions breakeven chart may not work well.
- ❖ Breakeven chart concentrate on breakeven level of production only while there are many important operations of business which are to be taken care to make business successful.
- ❖ In this chart curves are drawn as straight lines while in reality this may not be the case.

Growth of Firm

Any business grows in two ways

- ❖ Internal Growth:
  When the business increases its Production and activity level with the passage of time. This is called internal growth.

❖ External Growth: (Integration)
  When a business grows or expand through integration (i.e.
  Takeover or merger)
Takeover: When one business buys another business
Merger: When two businesses combine and become one
business.

Large scale production

Large scale production means production of goods in large
quantities. Basically it refers to large businesses, who deal huge
quantities of goods.

Economies of scale/Advantages of large scale production

❖ *Financial Economies*
❖ When a business becomes large it can be benefited by choice
  of wide sources of finance.
❖ *Technological economies*
❖ Large businesses can afford to buy latest technology and in
  this way minimized their costs and increase their productivity.
❖ *Marketing economies*
❖ Large businesses can afford to pay large sums for the
  advertisement and promotion of their products.
❖ *Professional economies*
❖ Large businesses can hire specialized people for different
  jobs e.g. marketing manager, chartered accountants, human
  resource manager etc.

Diseconomies of scale/ Disadvantages of large scale production

❖ *Management diseconomies*
❖ When a business become large, it will be more difficult to
  manage this large business.
❖ *Employees are de-motivated*

❖ Employees feel alienated and are de-motivated in a large business, as they think their performance will not be rewarded accordingly due to large number of employees.

External economies of scale/Advantages of whole industry being large

❖ **Cooperation:**
When different businesses producing identical goods are located near each other, the owners will be able to cooperate with each other in many management areas. They can help each other.

❖ **Availability of labour:**
Skilled labour will be more conveniently available in near about, due to the establishment of industry.

❖ **Ancillary firms:**
Many related firms locate their businesses near the industry because they can get more business from the industry.

❖ **Facilities are provided by the government:**
When many identical firms are located at one place and so make an industry, then government facilitates industry by providing many services to them like road, rail, dry port, government offices etc

Why small businesses exist and how they can survive?

Due to the following reasons small businesses survive even in the presence of large businesses.

❖ *Personalized services*
❖ Some businesses are of the nature where personalized are required by the customers e.g. barber shop, physiotherapist etc.

❖ *Customized services*
❖ Some business provide customized services to customers i.e. they provide goods as per customer's requirements. Due to this reason these business cannot be large.

❖ *Market size*
❖ Some markets are small due to which there must be small business. Large business will at small market is wastage of resources.

- ❖ *Location of the business*
- ❖ Some small businesses exist as they are located near to customer residences.
- ❖ *Personal will of the owner*
  A business may be small as its owner wants it as small.

Profit Maximization

What is Profit?

Profit is the positive difference between total revenue and total cost.

$$\text{i.e. } Profit = TR - TC$$

Profit per unit is the positive difference between Average revenue and average cost.

$$\text{i.e } Profit \ (per \ unit) \ or \ Average \ profit = AR - AC$$

Every Business wants to maximize its profits. It is the main objective of every business. At what level a business will have the maximum level of profit? It depends on the market situation. There are two types of Market situations.

- ❖ *Perfect Competition*
- ❖ *Monopoly*

Basic Rule is that Profit is maximum where MC(Marginal Cost) = MR (Marginal Revenue)

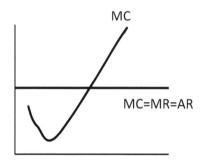

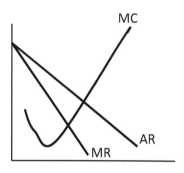

Under Perfect Competition   Under Monopoly

Types of Business Organization

Types of businesses:

There are many types of business organizations; depending on the way the owners of businesses organize resources to produce goods and services. And who owns the business?

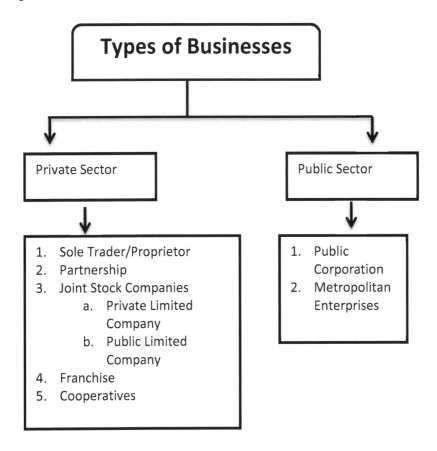

Private Sector:

All those businesses, which are owned and controlled by the people are called private sector.

Public Sector:

All those businesses which are owned and controlled by government are called as public sector.

Limited Liability:

It means, if the business is making losses and has failed and Business cannot pay its creditor, then owner/owners of the business will not be liable to pay this from its personal property. They will lose only the amount which they have invested in the business. This kind of liability is called limited liability.

Unlimited Liability:

It means, if a business goes failed and cannot pay its creditors. The owner/owners of the business will have to pay all the creditors even from their personal property. They must have to pay all the liabilities by selling business property as well as personal property. This kind of liability is called unlimited liability.

Sole Proprietorship:

Sole proprietorship is a one man business which is owned and controlled by only one person. Owner of the business has unlimited liability and is responsible of management of business as well as all profit and losses are born by him only. This kind of business organization has the following feature,

a) One person is the owner of the business
b) Owner has the unlimited liability
c) Whole capital is invested by one person
d) All profits and losses are of one person only.
e) The owner has to manage its business himself.

f) All business decisions are made by him.
g) No formal registration is required to establish this kind of business, So it is an unincorporated business.

Advantages:

1. There is secrecy in the business as the owner does not need to share its secrets with anyone else.
2. He is the only person who takes all decisions.
3. Owner can choose its working timing independently as well as its leaves or rest time.
4. Owner is not answerable to anyone.
5. Owner owns all the profits of the business.

Disadvantages:

1. Owner has the unlimited liability.
2. All losses go to only one person i.e. the owner of the business.
3. He cannot expand his business to a large level as it will be difficult to manage it alone.
4. He has the limited finance sources i.e. he cannot raise finance easily.
5. If he becomes ill or dies business will not continue.

Partnership:

Partnership is a business type in which minimum two and maximum twenty persons get together and run business together. They all contribute their capitals/investments and manage the business altogether.

Partnership Deed

Partnership deed means the agreement between the partners which may be written or verbal, but it should be in written form to avoid any future problems. Following are the most common contents of a sample partnership agreement.

1. Partners' investments
2. Partners' shares of profit and loss

3. Procedure of adding a new partner
4. Procedure of exit of an existing partner
5. Right and duties of all partners
6. Procedure of dissolution of partnership

Advantages

1. As compared to sole trader, it has more options of finance.
2. Losses are shared between the partners and all burden do falls on one person.
3. Management is shared between the partners so less responsibility to one person
4. Partners consult with each other while taking business decisions so it is easy to decide any matter.
5. There are more persons in ownership so there will be more ideas.
6. Business will not be stopped if anyone of them become ill or died
7. There are no legal formalities involved in registering this kind of business so easy to establish.

Disadvantages

1. There are conflicts most often between the partners.
2. Other partners are bound to the promise or agreement made by one partner.
3. Lack of trust between the partners.
4. These businesses do not survive for a longer period of time.
5. Less sources of finance available.
6. Unlimited liability of all the partners except some special cases.

Joint Stock Companies

Joint Stock companies are the businesses who are incorporated businesses (Properly Registered). Owners combine their investments in these businesses. These businesses are mostly large businesses. Capital invested in the business is called share capital. Ownership is separate from control. That is the owners are different people and the people who run and control businesses are different. Proper record is kept of the businesses as per law, and final accounts are submitted to registrar of the companies.

There are two types of joint stock companies

a) **Private Limited Companies**
b) **Public Limited Companies**

Private Limited Company:

In this form of businesses there are shareholders who contribute their investments in business capital. The shares of the company cannot be traded in the stock market. These can only be sold to family and friends. Proper records of the business transactions are required to be kept by law. Owners have limited liability.

Advantages:

1. Properly incorporated businesses, so that there are many benefits of incorporation.
2. Limited liability of shareholders
3. Comparatively large businesses as compared to sole trader and partnership.
4. Investors have more confidence in these type of businesses relatively.
5. Less chances of failure of the business.

Dis-Advantages

1. Shares cannot be traded in stock market
2. Business expansion is not possible to a major level.
3. Finance can be raised to a certain limit only.
4. Research and development cannot be conducted as it involves huge investment.

Public Limited Company:

In this form of business organization, there are shareholders who contribute their investment in business capital. Public Limited

Company can raise their capital as much as it can. Its shares can be traded at stock exchange. Maximum no of shareholders are unlimited. There is divorce in between its ownership and control i.e. a board of director control the company. Minimum one Annual General Meeting (AGM) of shareholders is necessary. In AGM shareholders vote the current board of directors to carry on working for the next year or not. Public Limited Company can advertise and invite shareholders to invest in the company.

Advantages:

1. Maximum no of shareholders are unlimited
2. Large sum of capital can be raised
3. PLC are mostly large companies who can conduct costly research and development.
4. Can invest in latest technologies which improves the quality of products and services,
5. Due to large scale of production can achieve economies of scale.
6. Very less chances of failure of the company.
7. Maximum no of sources of finance are available for the PLCs
8. Can form monopolies.
9. Can easily take over smaller businesses and so reduce their competition in the market.
10. Costly and more efficient and specialized ways of marketing can be adopted by the PLC
11. Limited Liability of all shareholders.

Disadvantages:

1. Much legal formalities in the formation and running of the company.
2. Real owners or founders can lose their control on the company as if majority share are bought by someone else.
3. There is no secrecy as all information is legally required to be public.
4. It is very costly to form a PLC

Franchise:

It's a form of business in which one business buys the rights or license of a famous brand or business to use that business's name and product to sell. Main purpose is that it is easy to establish and customers or people already knows the name of the business. Famous business who gives right or license is called Franchisor. The business who buys the rights or license is called franchisee. Franchise business is quick to setup and start earning revenues.

Advantage to Franchisee:

1. Easy and quick to setup
2. No need of marketing as the name is already known to people.
3. Profits may be earned from the very start of the business.
4. All products and its quality standards are known to people.
5. No need to design new products.
6. No need to do heavy market research.
7. Quick income starts on setting up the business.
8. All staff training will be provided from Franchisor.

Disadvantages to Franchisee:

1. Whenever the business wants to use its own name, it will have to start from zero.
2. A heavy amount is to be paid as license fee or rights fee.
3. A certain percentage may also have to be paid to franchisor from revenues.
4. All standards of franchisor must to be maintained.
5. Raw materials may also have to be bought from only franchisor.
6. Franchisor has the right to cancel franchising license at any time.

Cooperatives

Cooperative is an organization of businesses. Most commonly small businesses join cooperative to enjoy the purchasing economies and marketing economies which only large businesses can enjoy. Cooperatives are formed on the rule of mutual benefit.

Features:

1. Each member have right of one vote. It is not like PLC that as much shares a shareholder held, he has that much votes.
2. Decisions are made on majority basis.
3. Cooperatives are run by board of directors who are elected by the members.
4. Cooperatives are owned and controlled by the its members.
5. The members are the users or customers of the cooperative's products or services.

Advantages:

1. All member businesses can enjoy purchasing economies by having large discounts and cheapest possible prices.
2. All member businesses can enjoy marketing economies by having large budget marketing strategies which benefit all members collectively.

Disadvantages:

1. All members cannot have competitive advantages over each other as all members are getting and offering same prices of their products.
2. They individually cannot market their businesses on their name.

How Prices are decided (Demand & Supply)

How prices are decided (Demand & Supply)

Demand:

Willingness and ability of consumers to buy a good at a certain price is called demand

Law of Demand:

When price of a good falls its demand rises and when price rise its demand falls assuming that all other factors remain constant.

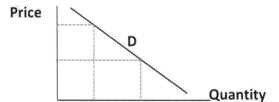

Shift in demand:

When demand changes due to factors other than price this change is called shift in demand.

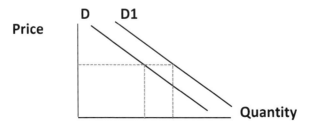

Factors effecting shift in demand:

Factors which effect shift in demand are also called as non-price factors. These factors are as following.

1. Fashion
2. Taste
3. Weather
4. Income tax
5. Substitute goods and complimentary goods

Supply:

Willingness and ability of producers to produce and sell a particular good at a certain price is called supply.

Law of supply:

When price rise supply rises and when price falls supply also falls assuming that all other factors remain constant.

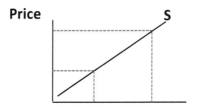

Shift in Supply:

When supply changes due to factors other than price, this change in supply is called shift in supply.

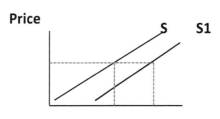

Factors effecting shift in supply:

1. Indirect tax
2. Prices of raw materials, Wage Rates and other manufacturing costs.

Equilibrium price:

Equilibrium price is that price at which both, quantity supplied and quantity demanded is equal to each other. This price is the stable price.

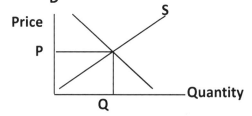

Dis-equilibrium:

Price of a certain good above or below the equilibrium price is called dis-equilibrium because it will not be stable price and eventually change. In the following figure we can see at price P1 which is above the equilibrium price, there is excess supply. Sellers will try to sell their goods by lowering the prices and eventually equilibrium price will establish. In the same way at price P2 there is excess demand which result in rise of price and eventually equilibrium price will establish.

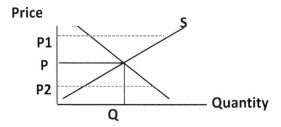

Effects of shift in demand over Equilibrium price:

Once equilibrium price has been established then it can only be changed when there is any shift in demand or supply. Here we consider the shift in demand. In the following figure we can see when demand curve shift upward to D2. New equilibrium is now at E2 where we can see price has arisen and quantity has also increased. In the same way if the demand curve shifts downward equilibrium price and quantity will also fall.

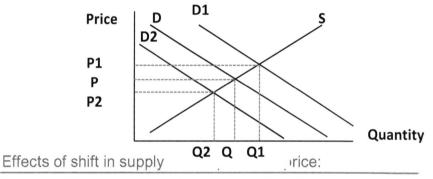

Effects of shift in supply ⋯rice:

Once equilibrium price has been established then it can only be changed when there is any shift in demand or supply. Here we consider the shift in supply. In the following figure we can see when supply curve shift upward to S2. New equilibrium is now at E2 where we can see price has fallen and quantity has increased. In the same way if the supply curve shifts downward equilibrium price will ⋯⋯ ⋯⋯ ⋯⋯ ⋯ 'll fall.

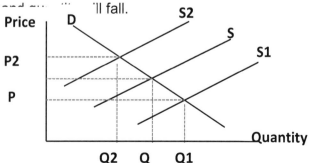

Price Elasticity of Demand:

Elasticity refers to responsiveness of demand. It means up to how much extent the demand is changed. Price Elasticity of Demand refers to the responsiveness of demand with respect to change in price of that particular product. Price elasticity of demand is measured by the following formula is

$$PED = \frac{\%\Delta Demand}{\%\Delta Price}$$

While $\quad \%\Delta D = \dfrac{change\ in\ quantity\ demanded}{Basic\ quantity\ demanded} \times 100 \qquad$ and

$$\%\Delta P = \frac{Change\ in\ the\ price}{Basic\ Price} \times 100$$

The answers of this fraction may of the following types

Unitary Elastic	Relatively Elastic	Relatively inelastic
PED = 1	PED > 1	PED < 1
e.g $\dfrac{25\%}{25\%} = 1$	e.g $= \dfrac{50\%}{25\%} = 2$	e.g $= \dfrac{25\%}{50\%} = 0.5$

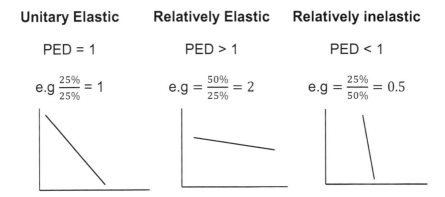

Perfectly Elastic **Perfectly inelastic**

$PED = \infty$ $PED = 0$

Factors effecting elasticity of demand:

1. No of substitutes
2. Time Period
3. Degree of Necessity or Luxury
4. Advertisement and promotion spending (Branding)
5. Permanent or temporary price change

How Price Elasticity of Demand is used in Price decisions:

Correct knowledge of product's PED is very helpful in making correct decisions of products price. In the following is the effect of different PED values on total revenue of the firm.

1. When PED = 1 (Unitary Elastic Demand)
   P↑ => TR/TE No effect , P↓ => TR/TE No Effect
   By increasing or decreasing the price of the products there will be no change in revenue because any change in price will be compensated by equal change in quantity demanded.
2. When PED > 1 (Relatively Elastic Demand)   P↑ => TR/TE ↓ , P↓ => TR/TE ↑

By increasing the price of the product there will be fall in total revenue of the firm and by decreasing the price of the product there will be an increase in total revenue of the firm.

3. When PED < 1 (Relatively inelastic Demand) P↑ => TR/TE ↑ , P↓ => TR/TE ↓

    By increasing the price of the product there will be an increase in total revenue of the firm. In the same way by decreasing the price of the product there will also a decrease in the total revenue of the firm.

Labor Market

Demand of Labour

It is the willingness and ability to hire an employee on a certain wage rate by an employer at a certain time.

Supply of Labor

It is the number of people willing and able to work on a certain wage rate in a country at certain time.

Wage Rate Determination

It is the wage rate where demand of labor and supply of labor is equal. It is the equilibrium rate or market wage rate.

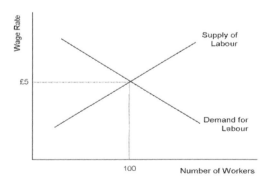

Factors effecting Demand of Labour

- Country's Economic Conditions
- Economic Structure changes
- Management
- Social Awareness
- Literacy Rate
- Govt. supply side Policies

Factors effecting supply of labour

- Job Security
- Size of business
- Skills required
- Literacy Rate
- Fringe Benefits
- Growth Rate of the Economy

Wage differentials in same occupation

- Education Level
- Experience
- Performance
- Loyalty and honesty
- Tenure in the firm

Wage differentials in different occupation

- Education Required
- Odd jobs
- Experience
- Mobility of labour
- Fringe benefits
- Skilled or non-skilled jobs
- Trade unions

Factors effecting choice of occupation

- Education required
- Experience required
- Mobility of labor
- Fringe benefits available
- Job security
- Trade union
- Location of the business
- Traveling involved in the job

How the Economy Works

Macroeconomics:

The study of how an economy works, is called Macroeconomics. It includes government level economic matters like inflation, unemployment, exchange rates, interest rates taxes etc.

National Output:

Total goods and services produced in a country are called as National Product.

National Income:

Goods and services are produced by employing all four factors of production like land, labour, capital, enterprise. These factors of production in return earn income in the form of salaries, rent, and profits. So national income can be measured by adding all the incomes earned in the country.

How economy works:

To understand the working of economy we assume a sample model. In this model we assume that in the country there are only households and firms. People live in households and work in firms. Same households people are the provider of factors of production to factories and they earn from there income in the form of rent, salaries, profits and interests. The same people spend their income on buying goods which are produced in factories.

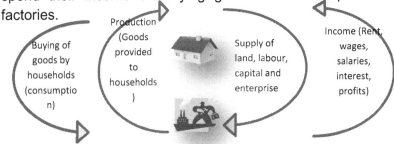

We can see from above picture that income and money flows in a circle which is called circular flow of income. Here we can also see that in our economy model there is no involvement of government and there is no discussion of imports and exports. We can also conclude from the above model that

National income = National expenditure = National output

But there are leakages and withdrawals in the economy in because peoples do not spend all of their income on buying goods and services as they have to pay taxes to government etc.

Leakages:

It means the money which goes out of the circulation in the form of taxes, savings, money spent on imported goods.

So we can say

National income (Y) = taxes (T)+ Savings (S)+ Imports (I)+Consumption expenditure (C)

As money goes out of circular flow. at the same time some money also injected in the circular flow which is called Injections.

Injections:

Money injected in the circular flow of economy may be in the form of Government expenditure, Exports, investments etc.

We can say

Aggregate demand = Consumption expenditure (C)+Investment (I)+Government Expenditure (G) +Exports (X)

Or

AD = C+I+G+X

Consumption Expenditure:

Money spent by the people from their income to buy factories outputs is called consumption expenditure.

Economy in Equilibrium:

Economy will be in equilibrium when leakages are equal to injections. It means the money which is going out of the economy and which is being injected is the same value.

Economy in disequilibrium:

Economy will be in disequilibrium when leakages and injection are not equal to each other it means some time leakages are more than injections which effect economy and sometimes injections are more than leakages.

Business Cycle:

This all ups and downs are called business cycle. Business cycle consists of booms, recession, slump and then again boom.

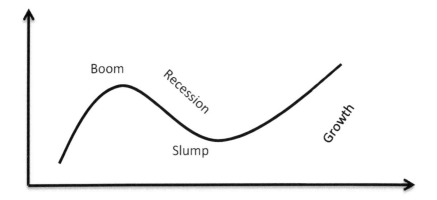

Booms

It will be there when national output or national income is increasing in real terms more than normal. There will be more consumer spending and so more aggregate demand Therefore producers will tend to invest more to increase production to meet aggregate demand. At last there come the point when all scarce resources will be fully employed and no more goods and services can be produced as a result there will be general price rise which is called inflation. Domestic goods will become costly and therefore people will start buying cheap imported goods. As a result demand of domestic goods will start to fall. Here booms breaks. As aggregate demand start to fall and production will also start to fall.

Recession:

It is when there is a fall in aggregate demand and fall in real output or production. I this situation firms will not wish to invest more to raise the production. Rather they will try to cut their expenses and lay off labour. Unemployment will increase and prices of goods will start to fall. National income will also fall.

Slump:

When recession prolongs for a longer time period it is called slump.

Growth

It is a period of time when demand is rising and that's why price level is also rising but it is covered by the increase in supply of goods. So the price rise (inflation) is controlled. GDP of the country is rising. Unemployment is falling.

The multiplier:

A change in aggregate demand can have widespread effect in the economy. Once the change has started it carry on and booms become bigger and bigger and slumps get deeper and deeper.

We can explain this in the following example;

Assume there is a large car manufacturing company in our country. If due to any reason people do not buy its cars or buy less cars this company will have to decrease its production and will try to cut its expenses by making redundant its employees, say 400 employees. This company will also reduce its order to parts manufacturing companies which will make these ancillary companies also to redundant their employees. In the same way it may become wider. Unemployment in the country will rise and the unemployed people will have no income to spend on goods and services. This will reduce the overall demand of all goods and services and which result in more unemployment.

We can see from the above example that how slumps get deeper and deeper and in the same way booms get bigger and bigger. This effect is called **multiplier** effect.

Crowding out:

During recession time period governments often try to increase aggregate demand in the economy by government spending which is a temporary arrangement to get rid of recession and to put economy on growth again. Due to increased government spending there is a decrease in unemployment and an increase in aggregate demand which makes prices to rise. As prices rises manufacturers and producer become interested to increase their production as well to earn more profits.

Drawback is that government spending must have to be paid off by borrowings or increasing taxes. When taxes increase it decreases private sector spending. This government strategy to get out of the recession is called **Crowding Out**.

Factors effecting consumption and savings:

1. The level of income:
   More will be the income more people will save and spend.
2. The government:
   If government lower taxes people will have more to spend and save.
3. The availability of saving schemes:
   More will be the saving schemes more options people will have to save and spend less.
4. Rate of inflation:
   As inflation rises people save more to protect the real value of their money.
5. Personal factors:
   Some people are more cautious and save while some people spend more and save less.
6. Interest rate:
   As interest rate rise people save more because they get more profit percentage on their savings.

Factors effecting investment:

1. Business optimism
   If the business environment in the country is very much favoring businesses i.e. production is increasing and there are increasing profits this will affect people and more people will come towards investing in business.
2. Interest rates
   when interest rate rise people borrow less from banks and so investment in businesses reduces. Borrowing becomes costly so people do not borrow as they have to pay more interest.
3. Technological advancement
   New advancements in technology encourage people to invest more in new technology as this increases production or productivity.
4. The government
   Government policies affect businesses both way that is encouraging policies will rise investments in businesses and discouraging policies will make people to reduce investments or with draw investment in the businesses.

Factors affecting demand for exports:

1. Income in foreign countries
2. The value of the local currency in terms of foreign currency
3. Interest rates

Economic Aims of Government

- Keeping low level of Inflation
- Keeping low level of unemployment
- Controlling Balance of Payment (BOP)
- Economic Growth

Economic policies to get economic objectives

Fiscal Policy

This is the policy through which a government balances its spending with tax collection. This policy includes deciding tax rates to be levied and the selection of goods and services to be taxed. This also includes decisions regarding spending on different areas of the economy of the country. This policy is used to control economic growth, consumer spending and economic structure of the country. There are two types of taxes which a government uses to collect revenues from public.

Categories of taxes

Direct Tax (Income Tax)

Direct taxes are those taxes which are levied directly on the incomes of the people. For example income tax, corporation tax, withholding tax etc

Indirect Tax (Value added tax / Sales Tax)

Indirect taxes are those taxes which are levied on the sales of goods and services. For example Value added tax or sales tax or import duties etc.

Types of taxes

Progressive tax

It is the type of tax whom rate increases with the rising level of income. For example Low rate of tax for lower income level and higher rate of tax for higher level of income

Regressive tax

It is the type of tax whom rate decreases with the rising level of income. For example high rate of tax is levied on lower level of income and low rate of tax is levied on high level of income.

Proportional tax

It is the type of tax whom rate remain fixed for any level of income.

Monetary Policy

This policy is managed and controlled by the central bank of the country. This policy includes the control of money supply and interest rate. This policy is usually considered as demand side policy. This policy is used to control the inflation rate, consumption expenditures and saving trends of the people and money supply in the market.

Effects of Monetary Policy

Increasing Interest Rate

When government increases interest rate following things are happened

- Borrowing by public is reduces
- Investment in new projects is reduced
- People tend to save more
- Economic Growth slows down
- Demand of goods and services is reduced
- People's spending on goods and services is reduced

Decreasing interest rate

When Govt. reduces interest rate following things are happened

- Borrowings by people increases
- Investment in new or existing projects rises
- People tend to spend more
- Demand of goods and services rise
- Economic growth rises/DGP Rises

Supply Side Policy

Supply side policies of the government, refers to those actions and decisions which help increase production of goods and services. It is mainly a supply side policy to increase supply. This policy includes following actions

- Opening of new college or training centers to produced skilled labour
- Providing assistance to small and medium size businesses
- Providing help and assistance to research and development
- Opening of new research and development centers
- Providing financial support to businesses
- Providing subsidies to new businesses

Macroeconomics – Inflation, Unemployment and Growth

Inflation:

Inflation refers to a general and sustained rise in the level of prices of goods and services.

Types of inflation:

Hyperinflation:

When prices rise at phenomenal rates and money becomes almost worthless. This is called hyperinflation.

Stagflation:

This is a situation when prices and unemployment both rises at the same time. It is a very dangerous situation because it means there is no more increase in production of goods and due to which supply is not increasing and on the other side demand is increasing which increasing the prices of goods.

Deflation

Deflation is the actual falling of prices which is a bad thing because falling prices of goods make producers to stop producing.

Disinflation

It is not falling of prices rather it is slowing of price increase or reducing inflation rate. It means that the speed of increasing prices is reducing.

Measuring Inflation:

Inflation is measured by calculating changes in prices of goods and services. Price change is calculated through the following formula;

%age change in price = $\frac{current\ price - old\ price}{old\ price} \times 100$

This %age change in price is normally shown by index number. This is the way to describe the change in just a simple number. For example if there is a change of 20%. The base year price is given a number 100 and so to represent the change of 20% the current year's number will be 120. It will be called as current year's index is 120.

Example:

Products	Weight	Base year price	Current year price
Clothing	20%	20	22
Food	40%	10	12
Transport	40%	8	10

RPI (Retail Price Index) = current year price/base year price x 100

Clothing   = 22/20 x 100 = 110%

Food   = 12/10 x 100 = 120%

Transport   = 10/8 x 100 = 125%

CPI of Economy= $\frac{(RPI\ x\ W)1 + (RPI\ x\ W)2 + \ldots (RPI\ x\ W)n}{Total\ Weigh}$

$= \frac{(110\ x\ 20) + (120\ x\ 40) + (125\ x\ 40)}{100}$ = 120

Inflation rate = $\frac{CPI-1}{100}$ X 100

So in the above example inflation rate will be as

$\frac{120-100}{100}$ $\square$ $100 = 20\%$

Causes of Inflation:

Demand pull inflation:

When there is an increase of demand of goods and there is no sufficient supply of goods. It will result in increase in prices of goods.

Cost push inflation:

It is when prices of raw materials or all the factors of production rises and that's why prices of goods have also to be risen. This kind of inflation is called cost push inflation.

Money supply:

Due to increase in money supply in the market prices also rises. Actually Government spend money for development and pay its costs from taxation and by printing more currency notes. When government pay this money it comes in hands of people and in this way they can buy more goods and services, hence this increases demand and make prices to rise.

Imported inflation:

When prices of imported goods rise it also effect prices of domestic goods and in this way there is an overall price rise which is called imported inflation.

Important definition:

NAIRU – (Non accelerating inflation rate of unemployment)

In response to rise in demand of goods supply needs to be increased as well by employing more factors of production. If there are no more factors of production to be employed that is all factors of production are fully employed. This situation is said as economy is at its NAIRU.

If there are unemployed factors of production then these can be employed to fulfill the demand of consumers and the prices will tend to rise very slowly. This situation will be said as economy is below its NAIRU.

When economy is above its NAIRU Prices will rise and with the passage of time its rate will also increase.

Cost of Inflation (Disadvantages of Inflation):

Inflation is good and bad both for country and consumers. Good will be for country only when there is very low inflation because it serves as an incentive and attraction for producers to produce more to earn more profits. In this way country's GDP increases. No doubt for consumers it is not good but they do not suffer so much because they are compensated with an increase in their incomes.

Inflation is bad when it increases at higher rates i.e. prices are increasing at higher rates say 10% or 20%. Inflation at high rates effect badly both to the country as well as individuals as discussed in the following.

Effects on individuals:

When prices of goods rise, the purchasing power of consumers reduces i.e. they can only buy less goods as compared to previous. We can say their **real income** falls. For Example if one person's income in terms of money was $100 and it could buy ten goods of $10 each. If each good's price rises to $20. Now it can only buy 5 goods with the same $100. It means person's real income has fallen to half.

Effects on economy:

When prices rise at a high rate demand of those goods will fall and as a result supply is increased. It makes producers to stop further production and lay off labour to reduce their costs. It makes unemployment to rise.

If country's inflation rate is higher than the neighboring countries it will become more difficult sell our products to those countries and it will result a fall in exports and rise in imports. This situation also makes country's balance of payment worsen.

Unemployment:

Unemployment means number of those people who are willing and able to work but cannot find work and are staying idle. Work may be their jobs or their own business.

Unemployment rate:

Unemployment rate can be find out in the following formula.

$$\text{Unemployment rate \%} = \frac{Number\ of\ unemployed}{Total\ Working\ Population} \times 100$$

Claimant Count:

Claimant count or jobseekers allowance is a count of all those people who are claiming unemployment benefits with the government's employment services provider department.

Types of unemployment:

Frictional unemployment:

This unemployment occurs when an employee leave one job and search for another job, and spend some time without job. This type of unemployment is called frictional unemployment.

Seasonal unemployment:

This type of unemployment occurs when demand of some goods and services is seasonal. i.e. people are on work when these goods or services production is in course and when there comes the off season employees are also laid off.

Cyclical unemployment:

This type of unemployment occurs when there is too little aggregate demand for goods and services in the country. It is when whole economy is in recession. i.e. there is a fall in the production of goods and services. It is a dangerous thing because it may prolong to many years.

Structural unemployment:

When over a number of years whole country's economic structure changes e.g. primary sector to secondary sector or to tertiary sector or it may be opposite. When this kind of change is set in it means that there are different kind of skills needed and people have to change them self and make them trained for the changing needs of jobs to make them able to be employed. Those people who do not make themselves trained and educated for the new requirements they become unemployed. This kind of unemployment is called structural unemployment.

Factors effecting unemployment:

Technological advancement:

Technological advancement has made a change in our day to day life. Now a machine can perform work of many people more accurately and more efficiently. That's why it is a main factor many of the jobs are not required now. While at the same time new jobs have been created related to these new requirements.

Trade Unions:

When trade unions force employers to raise wages and salaries, It makes demand for labour to fall and resulting in unemployment.

Unemployment benefits:

Unemployment allowance and other benefits to unemployed make unemployed people to not be interested to work. Even if they are provided a job they try to lose it again.

Employer's national insurance contributions:

Employer's National Insurance Contributions make it too expensive to employ workers.

Lack of job information prevents people from finding jobs:

Sometime people don't have complete information that where they can find a new job. So they remain unemployed.

The minimum wage has been set too high by the government and that's why demand for labour falls.

Sometime government fixes minimum wage. Mainly its purpose is to benefit employees and make them better off and to save them from employer's exploitation.

Immobility of labour:

Many people do not want to move from one place to another to join another job due to their families and friends. This is called immobility. This is why at sometimes it becomes difficult to decrease unemployment.

1. Occupational immobility

Peoples' inability to change their occupations as they are specifically trained and educated in certain field and that's why can do a particular work. They cannot adopt another field where more salaries or wages are being offered.

2. Geographical immobility

This refers to employees inability to move from one place to other e.g. to other city or abroad for better salaries.

Effects of unemployment/Disadvantages

Unemployment effects economy and people. It effects other working people or on job people as they have to feed them as well. With an increase in unemployment dependency ration increases.

It affects economy as government has to give unemployed benefits to make them survive and meet their necessities. This payment as unemployment allowances is paid from taxes which are collected from those people who are on job or doing their businesses. Government has to sacrifice other development and welfare projects. With an increase in unemployment demand for goods and services will fall and as a result production of goods and services will fall and this add to unemployment more.

Economic Growth

Economic growth means increase in the amount of goods and services produced in the country this year as compared to last year. If more goods and services are being produced it means there is economic growth.

Measurement of Economic Growth:

Production and sale of goods and services generate income for people in the form of rents, wages, salaries, interests and profits. So economists measure growth by calculating national income.

How to achieve economic growth

Economic growth can be achieved in the following ways.

1. Discovery of more new natural resources
    Discovery of more new natural resources make country to be able to produce more goods and services.
2. Investment in capital:
    Production of more capital goods like machinery and tools enhance country's ability to produce more consumer goods.
3. Technical progress:
    New inventions, better production techniques make country to produce more goods and services.
4. Improved Education and skills of labour
    Human resource of the country can be better off by training them and improving their skills and educating them new techniques.
5. Reallocation of resources:
    As a country develops, resources tend to move out of primary production and into manufacturing and services where large increase in output have occurred.

Advantages of Economic Growth:

1. Higher level of consumption of goods and services by the people
2. Higher level of output from less use of resources.
3. Higher level of taxes gained by the government.

Disadvantages of Economic Growth:

1. There is opportunity cost of growth. For example producing more capital goods may due to decrease in consumer goods.
2. More factories to produce more goods and services means less land available for parks and other recreational activities.
3. Economic growth means we are using up of our natural resources.
4. Technical progress means fewer jobs for human labour as machines will work at their place.

Macroeconomics – International Trade

Why country Specialize?

Country specializes because there are some goods and services which they can produce more efficiently and cheaply as compared to other countries.

Why countries trade?

There are three reasons that's why countries trade with each other.

1. Some goods and services they cannot produce due to any reason so they buy from other countries to fulfill their needs or they can produce and sell to those countries that cannot produce those goods.
2. A country can produce a particular good or service but it would be better to buy from other country because it would be more economical/cheap to buy from other rather to produce.
3. A country can produce some goods and services to sell them international market and to earn revenue.

Comparative advantage theory:

What is Absolute Advantage?

When one country is better in producing one particular good as compared to other country this will be said as it has an absolute advantage over other country in producing that good. One country may have an absolute advantage due to many reasons for example, country has naturally favorable environment to produce a particular good or it bears less cost in producing that particular good as compared to other country.

Application of Absolute advantage:

Mostly 2x2 model is used to explain Comparative advantage theory. We assume the following things to explain it.

a) There are two countries
b) Both producing only two goods
c) Both are employing half of their resources on the production of each product.

2x2 Model (Before specialization)

	Food (Units)	Clothing (Units)
USA	150	40
UK	50	100
Total Production	**200**	**140**

2x2 Model (After specialization)

	Food (Units)	Clothing (Units)
USA	150 + 150	0
UK	0	100 + 100
Total Production	**300**	**200**

2x2 Model (After specialization & Trade)

	Food (Units)	Clothing (Units)
USA	300-100=200 (100 exports to UK)	60 (Imports from UK)
UK	100 (Imports from USA)	200-60=140(60 Exports to USA)

Total Production	300	200

As you can see in the above model there are two countries USA and UK, both are producing only food and clothing. Both countries are employing half of their resources on food and half on clothing. But we can see that USA is better in producing Food as compared to UK while UK is better at producing clothing. So we can say USA has absolute advantage in producing Food and UK has an absolute advantage in producing clothing. It is very clear from the above table that after specialization both countries collectively producing more goods it means they are able to use their resources more efficiently. After specialization and trade both countries have more goods from both the categories.

Comparative advantage:

Assuming the 2x2 model assumptions, if one country is better at producing both the goods as compared to other then we will consider the opportunity cost comparison. In this way a country will have comparative advantage if it has less opportunity cost in producing a particular good.

Explanation:

Before Specialization:

	Food (Units)	Clothing (Units)	Ratio
USA	130	200	1:1.54
UK	50	150	1:3
Total Production	**180**	**350**	

After Specialization:

	Food (Units)	Clothing (Units)	Ratio
USA	130+65 (Increase)	200-100(reduction)	1:1.54
UK	0	150+150(Increase)	1:3
Total Production	**195**	**400**	

After Specialization and Trade:

	Food (Units)	Clothing (Units)	Ratio
USA	140	100+125(Imports)=225	1:1.54
UK	55	300-125(exports)=175	1:3
Total Production	**195**	**400**	

In the above stated 2x2 model we can see that USA has advantage and is producing more both goods as compared to UK. But when we compare opportunity cost we see that UK is better at producing Clothing as compared to USA. So UK will specialize in producing Clothing while USA will shift some of its resources to specialize in producing Food alternatively. In this way both the countries are able to produce more goods collectively using the same resources i.e. have become more efficient. After trading both countries will have more goods.

Exports & Imports:

Exports and imports of a country consist of visible trade and invisible trade. So the Balance of trade will be Net difference of value of Exports and imports.

Visible trade: It consists of exports and imports of physical things or goods.
Balance of visible trade = value of visible exports - value of visible imports

Invisible trade: It consists of exports and imports of non-physical things like services e.g insurance, banking, tourism and software etc. It also includes inflows and outflows of interest, profit, dividends and transfers like foreign aids etc.
Balance of invisible trade = value of invisible exports - value of invisible imports

Balance of Payments:

The balance of payments includes all the payments and receipts between the two countries. It consists of three types of accounts

a) Current A/C
b) Financial A/C
c) Capital A/C

Current A/C :

It consists of all the visible and invisible trade i.e. payments and receipts in connection with visible and visible exports and imports. Mainly it shows how well country is doing in international trade.

Sample Current A/C

	1991	1997
Visible exports	103939	163704
Visible imports	114162	184302
Balance of trade in goods (A)	**-10223**	**-20598**
Invisible exports	26955	49099
Invisible imports	31346	61777
Balance of trade in services (B)	**+4471**	**+12678**
Income balance (C)	**-1953**	**+15782**
Current transfers balance (D)	**-669**	**-6388**
Current A/C balance(A+B+C+D)	**-8374**	**+1474**

Financial A/C:

It mainly consists of short term investment inflows and out flows e.g. investment in capital, shares and loans.

Capital A/C:

It mainly consists of long term investments inflows and outflows which are paid for the change of ownership e.g. buying selling of houses, machinery and factories.

Some Important Definitions:

Direct inward investment:

When a foreign firm setup a factory, office or a retail outlet in our country, it is called direct inward investment. When a firm re-invests its profits which have not been given to shareholders, it is also included in direct inward investment.

Portfolio investments:

When some foreigner buys shares in our country or give loans to our country's company or individual. In the same way someone from our country buys shares in foreign country or give loan. These are all called portfolio investments in and out of the country. We can say these are short term investment.

How to correct a Balance of Payments Deficit:

Balance of payment deficit is resulted when our country's import's value exceed export's value. We can also say it as un-favorable balance. Balance of payment deficit can be corrected by many of the government actions.

Deflation:

By rising taxes and reducing government expenditures government can reduce aggregate demand (overall demand) which will result in decreasing prices of the goods. This is called deflation. In this way people will buy less goods whether these are domestic goods or imported goods. So imports will decrease and there will be more goods available to be export. This all will help to correct balance of payment deficit.

Interest rate:

When government increase interest rate it attracts investors from abroad to invest in the country and it increases inflows and reduces outflows and in this ways balance of payment is better off.

Protectionism:

It refers to government policies and legislation to stop or reduce imports to protect countries local industries and business. Government can impose custom, tariffs, embargo or quota to reduce or stop imports. When imports are reduced it will improve country's balance of payment.

Devaluation:

When government de-value its currency i.e. the exchange rate, it benefits exports of the country and reduces imports because due to devaluation exporters will get more money and importers will have to pay more for their imports.

Trade Barriers (Protectionism)

Government's actions to discourage and reduce or stop imports and to protect the local industry are called trade barriers and this policy is called protectionism. There are following trade barriers which a government may use.

Tariffs:

It's a tax which is imposed on imports. It raises prices of imported goods and so decrease demand of imported goods.

Subsidies:

A subsidy is a grant given by the government to manufacturers and exporters to reduce their cost and to make them able to offer competitive prices in the international market.

Quotas:

A quota is a limit on the number of imports allowed into the country.

Embargo:

Embargo is a complete ban on imports of certain goods for example dangerous drugs etc.

Why trade barriers are used (Reasons)?

Trade barriers are used due to following reasons.

1. To protect a young industry
2. To reduce unemployment
3. To prevent dumping: Dumping is when a country sells goods in another country below their cost of production.
4. To react other country's barriers to our exports
5. To prevent over specialization: Free trade encourages countries to specialize in the production of a particular product in which they have comparative or absolute advantage. But specialization in one or two products is dangerous.

Exchange Rates:

When we have to pay imports from other country we will have to buy that country's currency to pay them. In the same way to pay us for our exports our currency will be bought from the international market. This demand and supply of currencies determine the exchange rate of a particular currency, just like the price of good.

Exchange rate are described in pair form i.e. in term of another currency for example EUR/USD means price of one euro in US dollars. The rate will be described as 1.3900 which means one euro is equal to 1.3900 US dollars. This rate increases or decreases depending its demand and supply.

When exchange rate increases it is called **appreciation** of the currency and when rate decreases it is called **depreciation** of the currency.

Exchange rates may be managed by the government in the following ways.

1. Free Floating exchange rate
2. Managed or pegged exchange rate
3. Fixed exchange rate

Free floating exchange rate:

When currency's exchange rates are determined via market forces of demand and supply this will be called as free floating exchange rate.

Managed or pegged exchange rate:

This is when government manage exchange rates by interfering in the market. Government buys currency in the international market when its rates decreases and reached to a lower limit and sells when rates reached at an upper limit. In this way government keep rates in between upper and lower limit.

Fixed exchange rate:

This is when government fixes the exchange rate and it cannot be changed until government change it.

Factors effecting exchange rates:

1. Changes in the balance of trade in goods and services. When exports rise and imports decreases currency appreciates or vice versa.
2. Inflation : Due to inflation prices rises of the exports. If prices of exports goe on increasing as compared to import prices it will reduce exports and so exchange rate will appreciate.
3. Changes in interest rates: Higher interest rates attract inflows and discourage outflows and so exchange rate appreciate or vice versa.

4. The price of oil: Petroleum is a basic factor in the prices of goods and services. As petroleum prices rises it increase prices of our exports and so demand for our exports will fall and exchange rate will also depreciate.
5. Speculation: It means making profit by getting benefit of currency exchange rate appreciation or depreciation. i.e. when it is expected that currency will

What benefits exchange rate stability?

Exchange rate stability encourages trade, as sellers will be able to make future agreements for the sale of their goods and services. If exchange rates are not stable and are subject to severe fluctuation then it will be hard to give price rates of goods for a longer time even selling and buying will be difficult.

Dirty Floating:

This refers to government intervention in currency market to manage exchange rate despite allowing currency to float in many countries. When government think that exchange rates are too high it will sell currency in the international market of increase supply to decrease exchange rate or vice versa. This type of floatation of currency exchange rate is called dirty floating.

Advertisement

It is the processes of informing people about a product or services through different ways. There are two types of advertisements.

Informative Advertisement:

It is a type of advertisement where main emphasis is to give full information about the product.

Persuasive Advertisement:

It is a type of advertisement which tries to persuade the consumer that he really need the product and should buy it.

Quality of advertisement:

Advertisement should fulfill the AIDA model. AIDA model is a simple model of advert design. It stands for,

A – Attention: Advert should attract the attention of consumer.

I – Interest: Advert should create interest in consumer for the product.

D – Desire: Advert should raise desire to buy the product.

A – Action: Advert should make consumer to buy the product.

Market Structure

Monopoly

It is a situation when there is only one firm producing one or more particular product in the market and there is no competitor of this firm. In this situation this firm is called monopoly firm.

Features of monopoly

- Only one firm is in the market
- Firm is Price maker
- Generally monopoly is a large size firm
- Monopoly firms enjoy economies of scale
- There is no customer sovereignty
- No focus on quality of goods
- Mostly high prices are charged

Advantages to monopoly Firm

- Economies of scale
- No competition in the market
- Abnormal Profits are earned
- High prices are charged for the product
- Business size is mostly large
- Monopoly is a price maker

Disadvantages of monopoly

- Customers are price takers
- Poor Quality goods are available to be purchased
- No variety of goods
- No choice

Perfect Competition

It is a market situation when there are a large number of producers and large numbers of buyers are in the market. Homogeneous goods are being produced and supplied in the market. There is no barrier to entry and exit to the firms. Everyone has complete knowledge of the market and prices.

Features of Perfect competition

- Large number of producers and suppliers
- Large number of customers
- A lot of competition
- Everyone is price taker
- Homogeneous products
- No barrier to entry and exit
- Availability of High quality goods
- Availability of wide variety of goods

Advantages of perfect competition

- Lowest possible prices
- High quality of products
- Wide variety of goods available

- No Barrier to entry and exit
- No one can influence prices
- Everyone has complete information
- Most Efficient use of resources
- Quick response to customer demands

Disadvantages of perfect competition

- Only Normal profits can be earned
- Only that one can survive who has low average cost
- Producers have to compete with large number of competitors
- It is hard to survive in the period of recession
- Large capital investment needed to achieve economies of scale
- Small firms find it very difficult to survive in the competition
- Research and development is hard to conduct due to insufficient funds

Money

What is money?

Money is some-thing which is generally acceptable as a medium of exchange for the exchange of good and services.

Types of money

- Currency Notes
- Coins
- Cheques
- Credit Card
- Debit Card
- Traveler's Cheques
- Prize Bonds
- Treasury Bonds

Functions of money

- Medium of exchange
- Measure of value
- Means of payment
- Means of deferred payments
- Store of value

Characteristics of good money

- Generally acceptable
- Legal tender
- Durable
- Scarce
- Portable

Banks

Central Bank:

Central bank is the main bank in the country. It is a government's bank and deals with government's payments and receipts and loans etc. It also serves as an authority to monitor banking system in the country.

Functions of Central Bank

Support government's fiscal policy

Central bank supports government fiscal policy by giving all related data and monitoring system.

Prints new currency notes

Central bank has the sole right to print currency notes and make coins.

Borrow money from open market functions

Central bank can borrow money from market functions to reduce money supply in the market and in the same way it can increase money supply in the market.

Looks after government's revenues and spending.

Central bank look after government accounts in course of payments and receipts.

Monitor banking system

Central bank monitor banking system in the country. It makes rules and regulation for other private commercial banks. It also approves new banks for operations. It monitors their functions. Central bank also make loans to commercial banks when they need it to save them from default.

Controls monitory policy

Central bank controls interest rate of the country. Central bank reduces or increases interest rates in the country as per requirement to help economic growth in the country.

Commercial banks

These provide banking services to businesses and consumers through a network of branches. These banks are in businesses to make profit for their owners. They are usually public limited companies owned by share holders.

Functions of commercial banks

Keeps money of their consumers

These banks keep customer's money with safety through different types of accounts. Customers can open currents accounts as well as deposit accounts with these banks.

Help their customers to make and receive payments

These banks provide services to customers to make and receive payments through cheques, Debit cards, credit cards, online transfers and demand drafts.

Lend money to customers

These banks lend money to customers on their requests and after going through verification procedures. In return banks earn interest from customers. Banks also provide leasing and hire purchase services for their customers.

Provide many other services.

Banks provide many other services to their customers for example discounting, letter of credit, money transfers in between different countries etc.

Market Failure

What is Market Failure?

Market Failure refers to a situation when free market economy does not work as per its rules. That is the market forces of demand and supply are not working. Examples of market failure are as follows,

1. Creation of pollution
2. Formation of monopolies
3. Production of dangerous good (Tobacco etc)
4. Over Production (of addictive goods like alcohol)
5. Under Production (of merit goods like education)

What is Private Cost?

Private cost is the cost of producing goods and services, which comprises of all the expenditures made by the firm during the course of production process.

What is External Cost?

External Cost refers to the damages incurred by the firm in due course of production process on its surroundings, i.e. society and environment. For example Pollution, (Noise, Air, Water) or lose beauty of the area etc.

What is Private Benefit?

Private Benefit is the revenue and income of the firm which it gain from the sale of good or services. For example Profits etc.

What is External Benefit?

External benefit means the benefits to society or environment which are caused by the firm's production activity of goods or services. For Example, Employment for the people of surrounding area, the goods and services which the people are consuming.

What are Externalities?

The term externality refers to the effects of business activity on the surroundings and society. These effect may be negative or positive. Positive effects are called as positive externalities and negative effects are called as negative externalities.

Social Cost:

Total of private cost and external cost is called social cost. (SC=PC+EC)

Social Benefit:

Total of private benefits and external benefits is called social benefit. (SB=PB+EB)

CBA (Cost Benefit Analysis)

Governments are more concerned with the welfare of the society that's why they are more concerned with social cost and social benefits. For this purpose they perform cost benefit analysis. To correct the disequilibrium government uses taxes and subsidies as a tool to correct the balance.

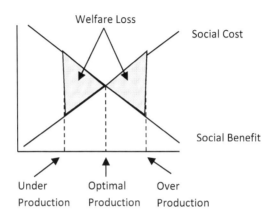

Population and Economy:

Factors Effecting Population:

Birth Rate

It refers to the number of births per 1000 people in a country in a year.

Death Rate

It refers to the number of deaths per 1000 people in a country in a year.

Migration

It refers to the net difference of Immigration and Emigration of a country in a year.

Immigration

It refers to the number of people coming into the country in a year.

Emigration

It refers to the number of people leaving the country in a year.

Factors Effecting Birth Rate:

Customs and traditions

Customs and traditions of society influences a lot on birth rate of a country. E.g early marriages and more births etc.

Religion

Religion is a very strong element in birth control. As religions encourages more populations. So that's why peoples having stronger beliefs in religion follow this encouragement.

Literacy

Literacy is a big factor in birth rate of any country. More literate is the population of the country more they will be conscious about family planning.

Early Marriages

In under developed or developing countries it is a custom of the society to early marriages of girls. Which increases the birth rate and so population too.

Family Planning Awareness and contraception

Now a day's most of the countries are running family planning awareness programs to help reduce the birth rate of the country.

Trend of women working in a society

In most of the societies now there is a growing trend of women working in different jobs. This trend makes them to care more about their career first.

Technology

Due to advancement in science and technology now a days health facilities are getting better and better day by day.

Health Conditions

Due to the betterment of health conditions birth rate is increasing and infertility rate is reducing.

Standard of living

Rising incomes and rising level of standard of living making people more mature and sensible and more aware of family planning.

Factors Effecting Death Rate:

Health facilities

Better Health facilities reduces the death rate of the country

Standard of living

Better standard of living makes people to spend neat and clean and healthy life keeps them healthier. If standard of living of the people in a country is getting better the death rate will also reduce.

Economic condition of country

Better economic conditions of the country makes people's standard of living better and make them able to get better health facilities resulting in a reduced death rate.

Govt. Support and welfare policies

Govt. policies towards providing welfare and health facilities are a major factor in reducing death rate of the country.

Advancement in Medicines

Due to advancement in science and technology there are new discoveries in the field of medicines which have reduced death rate of the countries.

Factors Effecting Migration:

Country Economic Conditions

If a country is economically strong people will try to move to that country to earn more income

Govt. Policies

Govt. Policies play a vital role as a factor in the migration. If govt. policies are supportive and are towards growth of the economy. There will be more immigration or vice versa.

To get higher Education

Many people move to other countries to get higher and better education.

Living Standard

Better living standards in a country attract more people from other countries.

Availability of Earning Opportunities

Due to growth and better economic conditions in a country more people move into the country to enjoy better income earning opportunities.

Availability of clean water

We can see in the history that peoples always gather to live near clean fresh water sources like alongside the rivers and canals or lakes. This is still a major factor.

Weather conditions

People moves away from the extreme weather condition places so this is also a factor influencing migration.

Population Pyramid

It is a graphical presentation of population distribution age wise and gender wise of a country at any particular time. This pyramid reveals a lot of information about the population structure of the country. For example mortality rate of infants, birth rate, death rate, standard of living and economic conditions etc. Here is a sample of population pyramid in the following.

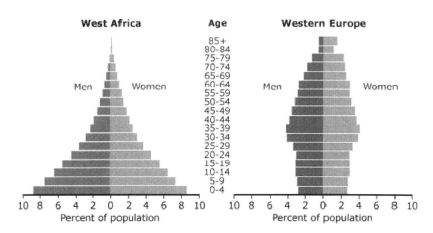

In the above Fig you can see that there is a difference between the two pyramids of both the regions. Pyramid of Western Europe is showing that there is a low birth rate and infant survival rate is high and death rate is very low. This all indicates that there is prosperity and standard of living is high and there is high literacy rate.

While on the other hand pyramid of West Africa shows that there is high birth rate and mortality rate is also very high that's why new birth do not survive to adult age. This shows that there is a low living standard and low economic conditions and eventually there is low literacy rate.

ABOUT THE AUTHOR

Hassaan Ahmad is an Author, Teacher and Entrepreneur from Faisalabad, Pakistan. He is teaching GCE A Levels Accounting, Economics and Business for more than 15 years and has produced excellent grades. He has served in a variety of organizations including educational institutes, Manufacturing concerns and service providers. He has not only theoretical experience as well as practical experience of the real environment. Being an entrepreneur, he is running his own business successfully.

Linkedin: https://pk.linkedin.com/in/hassaanahmadkhan

Facebook :   http://www.facebook.com/hassaanahmadkhan

Twitter: @hassaanahmadk

Web: www.hassaanahmad.com , www.bizacademia.com

Printed in Great Britain
by Amazon